CW00494084

# *How To Write A Groom's Speech*

*Rob Bartley*

Copyright © 2021 Rob Bartley at Speechful Publishing
All rights reserved

No part of this book may be reproduced, or stored in a retrieval system, or transmitted in any form or by any means, electronic, mechanical, photocopying, recording, or otherwise, without express written permission of the publisher.

Cover design by: Graphicsangela
Printed in the United Kingdom

*This book is dedicated to my beautiful wife - for, without her, I would never have had to write a Groom's speech.*

# CONTENTS

Appendices



Acknowledgements

# CHAPTER 1

## ISN'T IT ALL ABOUT THE BEST MAN'S SPEECH?

When I first got engaged to my incredible wife Helen - writing a Groom's speech was at the bottom of the list of things to do in preparation for the wedding - we had to arrange a venue, caterers, photographer, videographer, send out invitations, discuss awkward family politics, the list goes on.

However, once those were sorted (i.e. the future wife was handling them), I had some time to think about the speech and discovered that there wasn't much advice available for a discerning Groom - it seemed to be all about the Best Man's speech.

The Best Man has hundreds of books and online articles to gain useful insight and structure for their speech but there is very little for a Groom.

You may be wondering why a Groom needs to prepare a good speech - surely they just need to thank everyone and say how much they love their wife. After all, it is up to the Best Man to be interesting and funny.

I have been to many weddings where that is just the case and I only remember the Best Man's speech - I have forgotten most of those Grooms speeches. You don't want to be one of those forgotten ones now do you?

If you want your speech to be remembered by your friends and family for years to come (for all the right reasons of course), then you have done the right thing by picking up this book.

Think about what you want from your speech. Do you just want it to be over? I felt like that at the start, but then I came round to the idea that you can make it light-hearted, funny and you may even surprise a few guests who are just expecting a run-of-the-mill grooms speech.

The Groom's speech is also a great opportunity for you to say how much you love your friends and family and are thankful for what they have done for you throughout the years. It can be tough for people to express their feelings in everyday life so why not use this opportunity to express them in front of everybody. You can finally let those man-feelings out!

If you are lucky like me, your wife may have even convinced you to spend a small fortune on a videographer. This allows you to watch it back whenever you please. You may even let loads of strangers watch it on YouTube (See Appendix).

Standing up and speaking to a large group of people is very daunting, even if it is your nearest and dearest, and so it is extremely important to be fully prepared. Being prepared will help wash those nerves away.

As the old adage goes "fail to prepare, prepare to fail".

By purchasing this book you have taken the first step to avoid failure and together we can create a structured speech that will help reduce your anxiety and allow you to speak with confidence in one of the most important speeches in your life.

Straight after finishing my own Groom's speech, I had my parents saying it was the best Groom's speech they had ever heard. I of course just thought that was parental bias. At least Mummy had my back!

However, within a few days of the wedding, I had a few friends ask for hints and tips with regards to their own speeches. This made me think that I had a few good ideas that I could share about the process of writing a Groom's speech.

When I first set about writing my own speech I couldn't dream of such feedback. I had a lot of trouble on where to start, how to structure it, and what the content should be. I decided it was going to be a lot easier to break down the speech into focused sections which this book has outlined for you - in easy to read step-by-step chapters.

You should be writing this speech at least a month before the wedding but preferably longer. Make sure you have a pen or, like I did, the notes app on your electronic device, to take the themes from this book and start bullet-pointing the stories, the thanks, and the jokes. These will be personalised about your friends, family, and of course your future wife.

I have included excerpts from my own wedding speech. These are provided throughout the book as an example of what you could write. These are time-stamped, so you can use the YouTube video and see how I spoke that part of the speech. A link is provided in the Appendix or simply search for the following on YouTube:

'Rob Bartley Grooms Speech'

Feel free to use the timestamps as you read the book or you can watch the speech in its entirety. Should take you less than 20 minutes, which is approximately the amount of time your speech should be - aim for between 15 to 20 minutes.

My speech is a helpful example but your speech must be 100% yours. Your experiences, your stories, your jokes. Well - I may let you use a joke or two of mine, that's up to you though.

In chapters 9 and 10 I have also given some practical advice and a reliable process for how to prepare for the wedding day and the speech. The content of your speech may be dynamite, but if you haven't prepared correctly it could all be for nothing.

I have been in your position before and I understand the pressure - all it takes is the tips from this book and a lot of preparation and you will be well on track to creating a truly memorable speech.

Let's get started!

# Chapter 1 - Recap

- The Groom's speech can be just as funny and entertaining as the Best Man's
- Fail to prepare, prepare to fail
- Have a pen and paper or your device ready to jot down ideas for content

# CHAPTER 2

## TRADITIONAL WEDDING SPEECHES

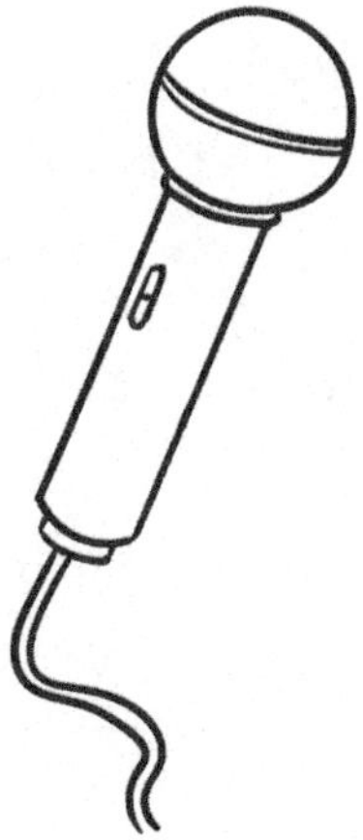

There are three traditional wedding speeches which tend to happen in this order:

- Father of the Bride's Speech
- Groom's Speech
- Best Man's Speech

Recently though I have seen several Brides and Maids of Honour now making a speech - although this may not be typically traditional in the UK, it is popular in America and becoming more popular across the globe.

If you know anyone preparing for any of these other speeches, keep an eye out for future book releases from the Speechful™ range.

For simplicity, I will be referring to the "Bride" or "Wife" throughout this book, but of course, weddings can have two Brides, two Grooms, and everything in between, so the term Bride here simply refers to the partner you are about to marry whatever their gender orientation is.

Below is the traditional content of each speech:

## Father of the Bride

This speech tends to focus on the Bride and their experiences growing up - a time before you even knew your future wife.

It may be advisable to have a conversation with the father of the Bride, or whoever will be speaking on their behalf, to understand the content of their speech - you want to try and avoid going over anything they may already be talking about - it is unlikely but worth that quick conversation.

You are next after this speech so you may well be feeling very nervous, but you really need to concentrate and listen to the father's speech. When it comes to you thanking them, try and refer to something they said. There was no speech before mine at my wedding so I managed to avoid this nervy period, but it is likely that you won't be so lucky, so listen intently.

For example, they are likely to mention handing over the responsibility of looking after their daughter, which is very traditional. A great little opener for you would be to acknowledge this:

*"Thank you for your kind words John, and of course I promise she is now in very safe hands"*

You could even lift up your hands up as you say it in a corny gesture - it's a good icebreaker and will get a few chuckles in the crowd, relaxing both them and you. However, that is just one option for an opener - see Chapter 4 for further options.

## Groom

All to be revealed in this book!

## Best Man

The most anticipated speech of the wedding.

There is quite a lot of pressure to be funny in this speech which may make you think that you don't have to add humour into your own speech.

I think differently here - you are with your closest friends and family so why not be jokey with them in your speech. Having a sense of humour is endearing to everyone and you can win over all the guests by being unexpectedly funny throughout it.

The Best Man will mostly focus hilariously on you and your embarrassing stories. They may even touch on how you met your other half.

Again you may wish to speak to your Best Man to get the gist of his speech (he, of course, won't tell you the details - it would ruin the surprise on the day!), but you can maybe ask him if he is covering the story of how you met, or if that is a green light for your speech.

Apart from that element, there should be minimal crossover as you are unlikely to tell embarrassing stories about yourself in your speech (or maybe you might - see later chapters).

You should actually aim to make your speech funnier than the Best Man's - as your speech progresses and the laughs are getting louder and louder, you want your Best Man to cry nervous tears, as he simply cannot follow such a perfect speech. OK maybe I went a bit far there, but you do want your speech to be at least on par with that of the Best Man's.

I believe my Best Man started his speech with the words "How do I follow that?!" as his opening line. That was a good feeling to have. (Annoyingly he did do a superb job on his speech, but of course, I would say mine was funnier).

## Bride's / Maid of Honour Speech

These are relatively new to the UK but quite popular in the US.

The Bride's speech is very similar to the Groom's

albeit a few less thank yous and a few more embarrassing stories about the Groom.

Also unsurprisingly the Maid of Honour's is similar to the Best Man's so there is no need to cover similar ground but maybe acknowledge that these speeches also exist and you may wish to think about where you want yours to sit in the line-up.

This is a personal choice but I would advise going just before the Best Man's speech which should be the final speech of the wedding.

The main aim of understanding the other speeches is to avoid going over the same material. Always have that thought in the back of your mind when writing your notes and ideas down. Only repeat something if you have a funnier, alternative side to a story!

One final tip is that the speeches are traditionally done after the meal. In my experience, doing them before means they are over earlier, so you have less time to build up those pesky nerves. It also means you are more likely to enjoy the food you have probably spent a fair amount of money on. Lastly, you are more likely to be sober so you can get those all-important words out in the right order.

Three great reasons for getting the speech done nice and early!

With that now established I think it is time to get the basics down.

# Chapter 2 - Recap

- Traditional wedding speeches include the Father of the Bride, The Groom's Speech and the Best Man's
- The Father of the Bride will focus on the Bride's early life
- The Best Man will focus on you - the Groom
- You want to try and not go over the same points that those other speeches will
- Try and arrange the speeches for before the meal

# CHAPTER 3

## THE BASICS

Having an idea of the basics will help you structure the content and will guide your thinking when we go through each section in the later chapters.

The basics, clearly laid out, allows you to avoid repetitiveness and it will help create a story that your wedding guests will be enthralled by.

Below is a list of what you need to include:

- Opener
- Acknowledging the Bridesmaids & Groomsmen
- Thanking the Parents
- Telling your new Bride how much you love them

These are the four key elements that make up a traditional Groom's speech. These have to be in your speech but if you rigidly stick to only those basics, that is far too simple. Your speech will be added to the long list of forgettable Grooms' speeches. Don't be forgettable - be unforgettable!

Here are some optional but I believe essential extras:

- Thank the whole room in the opener

- Bridesmaids - talk about each of them individually
- Groomsmen - talk about each of them individually
- Parents - talk about each of them individually (you get the idea)
- New Bride - tell a couple of funny stories before the lovey-dovey element

So although the basics are there, go into more detail. The devil is in the detail after all!

Those guests that you pick out and address individually will appreciate it so much more.

You can create a rapport and talk about that individual's characteristics that the rest of the crowd know, recognise and relate to. Even if they don't know that person it can be fun for the audience to find out new and funny things about those in your firing line!

Lastly, with regards to the Bride, your guests are there for just you two - so give them a little insight into your pre-married life! Unless you have signed up to Married At First Sight of course - if you have done that then a psychic may have better advice for you than this book!

Use these basics to form the outline of your speech. You can change the order of the Bridesmaids, Groomsmen, and Parents but always thank the room at the start and always end on your new Bride.

Each of the above has its own chapter dedicated to ensuring you write a speech that not only includes the basics, but also those essential extras that will make the difference.

You may have an idea of the general content of what your speech is going to include, and it is a good idea to have some bullet points with those ideas written down. The rest of this book will tell you how to structure those thoughts and put them in an order that flows, covers all the ground you need to, and ends in a loud applause for your efforts.

Now let's move on to one of the most important elements of the speech - The Opener!

# Chapter 3 - Recap

- There are a few basics for the speech:
    - Opener
    - Acknowledging the Bridesmaids & Groomsmen
    - Thanking the Parents
    - Telling your new Bride how much you love them
- Talk about each person individually
- Give the guests an insight into your pre-married life

# CHAPTER 4
## THE OPENER

The Opener of your speech is so important as it sets the tone for the remaining time you are speaking. You want to grab the audience's attention, make them feel at ease and if possible make them laugh. You certainly don't want them yawning from the start.

With that said though, we do need to discuss what to avoid first before I can advise what should be done.

I am hoping you already know you shouldn't open the speech with:

*[Producing a slice of toast] "And now, a toast."*

But let's think about the more subtle mistakes:

## Stock Jokes

It can be very tempting to go straight into a joke and to even use what I call a "stock joke", which is a well-known gag or something that is quite easily searchable on the internet.

The temptation arises from you believing that this is an easy way to get a quick first laugh and set you at ease, but the reality is half the guests would have heard it before and the other half won't find it that funny.

In all honesty, I was extremely tempted to start my speech with:

*"I am not usually good at public speaking - I normally piss pronounce my worms"*

Fans of The Office UK would be cracking up at that but that's a niche crowd. So I scrapped that idea - even though I am chuckling about it now as I write it.

Make sure you have all the guests in mind when thinking about the Opener.

Cheap laughs are not what you are after, and I have helpfully included some examples of these no-go jokes in Chapter 11.

Admittedly they are funny when you read them to yourself but keep it that way - your speech's comedy is going to be intelligent and linked to individual guests at the wedding, not ones that have been used a thousand times at a thousand weddings. Show your guests that you are one of a kind!

## Apologising

Another way you should not start your speech is to apologise to the guests. You may be nervous and want to lower the guests' expectations, so when you end up doing well they are surprised.

This tactic just has the opposite effect. If a speaker apologises it just makes the audience feel worried for you and more focused on your demeanour than your words. Openers like:

*"Apologies, I don't speak in front of large crowds often..."*

*"Erm, right, erm, let's err, let's get started"*

*"I'm sorry - like the Best Man's penis, I will try and keep this short"*

Not sure how that last one got there - think that needs to be added to Chapter 11 - Jokes to Avoid. See the revised edition of this book.

Those first two openers will diminish the value of your speech immediately and the confidence the audience has in you when you first stand up is immediately lost.

Now you know what not to do, let's move on to what you should be doing.

Below are a few ideas to what should be included in the opener:

## Say Thanks

I said in The Basics chapter that you need to thank all of your guests. This should be done immediately and only forms the first couple of sentences of the Opener.

Your guests will most likely have paid a fair bit of money to attend the wedding - travel, accommodation, a new suit or dress. They will have also likely purchased you a gift or contributed to your honeymoon. You need to acknowledge that but subtly - don't mention the money that's for sure, but say something along the lines of:

*"I would first like to say thank you to all of you for joining us on this special occasion. I know how much effort you have all made to be here so my wife...*

(pause and smile - this is the first time you have called her your wife in front of everybody!)

*and I just want to say we truly appreciate you all being here."*

This is an honest and heartfelt thank you to everyone and should get some wolf whistles and claps when you mention your new wife for the first time. You will probably find it weird calling her your wife - I still do several years later!

## Build Rapport

Next, you want to build on that initial thank you and create a connection with the audience.

This can be done in several ways - you are all in the same venue, you have all experienced the same wedding ceremony, eaten the same food (if you're doing the speech after the meal) and seen that garish dress one of the aunties is wearing. You could talk about any of those things as everyone has experienced them.

*"If anyone gets lost, please follow Aunty Norma - you can't miss her"*

OK - maybe leave Aunty Norma's dress sense out of your speech but any other shared experiences are fair game.

For the main part of my Opener, I decided to mention where people had travelled from as our wedding was in a location which involved a fair bit of travel for everyone. Therefore I felt this would build some common ground between me as the speaker and the guests as the listeners.

At my wedding I had people from all over the UK and some international guests - so I put out some special mentions to those who had travelled far. Then for a quick laugh, I said a special thank you to those who had come from the Isle of Wight (travelling to the "mainland" is a big deal to them!).

Here is an excerpt from my speech:

*"Right - here we go. Thank you to everyone for coming, it's an incredible effort. We've had people from Sheffield, Manchester, Germany. We've even had people from the Isle of Wight! Absolutely insane. Helen always told me about the three-lane motorways and the big roundabouts so you've been really brave. Respect. Respect for coming, so thank you very much."* **00:19**

As you can see - this hit all the right thank you notes and encouraged cheers from those groups of people who travelled from those specific locations. It also got some laughs from the Isle of Wight guests and the other guests who know that Islanders can get a bit spooked about coming to the "Mainland".

This built common ground between everyone and straight away I had everyone engaged in the rest of what I had to say. This quick engagement set everyone at ease and showed that I wasn't too nervous, allowing the guests to be invested in the rest of my speech.

In the video, you may notice my voice does falter a little on a couple of the words, and that is natural when you start - take a breath and compose yourself.

Now is the time to get your notebook or device out and jot down some ideas about what you will put in your opener. Note how are you going to say thanks and what common ground you are going to use to build rapport.

Now let's move on to the body of the speech and give those special mentions to the wedding party.

You can talk about the Bridesmaids, Groomsmen, and Parents in any order you want. In my speech, I wanted to build to the most important, so I started with the Bridesmaids. No offence to any of them if they happen to read this!

That is where the next chapter begins - The Bridesmaids.

# Chapter 4 - Recap

- Don't use a stock joke for an opener
- Don't apologise - it devalues your speech
- Thank all guests for attending
- Build rapport with the guests by finding common ground
- Set yourself and the audience at ease by being confident

# CHAPTER 5
## THE BRIDESMAIDS

The Bridesmaids, however many there are, all mean something to your new wife and so it is crucial you thank them individually. Too many Grooms say the following:

*"Thank you to the Bridesmaids for looking after my wife this morning and don't they all look great"*

And that's it. That's all they will say about the Bridesmaids and move on. Unless there is a speech from the Bride thanking them, this wide-sweeping comment is not enough.

The Bridesmaids have not only supported your wife on the morning of the wedding and made sure she got to the ceremony (mostly on time), but they have also been there to support her throughout her life. This should have some recognition and your speech is the place to do that.

Also, there is something in it for you. Just picture this - you give a great speech about the Bridesmaids that they cherish and remember forever (women are good at this). You then get into a little tiff with your new wife so she gets on a call with her best friends who happen to be Bridesmaids:

Wife: *"Rob's only gone and just pied me off for his mates and gone down the pub"*

Bridesmaid 1: *"Oh leave him alone he is allowed some pal time"*

Bridesmaid 2: *" Yeah - it's only the pub for a drink"*

Bridesmaid 3: *"Speaking of drinks - didn't he give us a lovely toast in his Groom's speech"*

See how that all worked out in your favour? A superb Bridesmaid section gets you in their good books for a long time.

Firstly - name them all - it shows you actually remember them! It will also likely get you a small cheer as it did in my speech:

*"I'm going to go to bridesmaids first - we've got Jo, Lacey, Louise, Saffron, Pippa & Sarah. I must say it's an absolutely incredible dress, they have all done it in a unique style and it looks amazing, you all look gorgeous."*
***00:48***

The subtle difference between the generic shout-out and what I said above is that I addressed each Bridesmaid by their name and I went into detail on the dress, not just "they all look great".

Next, I surprised the Bridesmaids by talking about them individually - they were probably expecting just the first shout out.

The tricky part is that you may not know all of

them that well, but in my opinion that doesn't matter. Over the time you have known your wife, you hopefully would have observed her with the Bridesmaids or she would have told you some stories about them. This is the material you can use to thank each of them individually.

If you are truly struggling to think of anything to say you can simply ask your wife if there is anything she would like you to include.

Below are a couple of examples from my speech where I specifically thanked some of her Bridesmaids:

*"Louise - whenever she comes to your salon... she makes Helen look gorgeous, every time she looks amazing. You share a love for cheese, wine, generally all the bad foods and Craig David shots. Incredible"* **1.28**

*"Next we have the maids of honour; Firstly Sarah, you have been Helen's best friend forever (BFF) and you organised some fantastic hen dos - Helen had an awesome time. I really appreciate the fact that you can keep Helen on the phone for about four hours at a time - so I can play my PlayStation. Keep that up"* **02:56**

As you can see for Louise - I mentioned things that both Louise and my wife enjoy - it got some wide smiles from both of them. Also in the video, you will see I ad-libbed a couple of other lines that went off on a bit of a tangent talking about milk-shakes. Random I know, but it got some laughs. If some other ideas come to your mind while you are speaking - don't be afraid to say them - these can sometimes get you the best audience engagement. Just remember though - try to stay on track (prompt cards will help you do this - more on that later).

With Sarah, I went for a different approach and used my own observations. The fact she has such long conversations with my wife shows they are great friends but also allowed me to have some gaming time - essential in any relationship. Again this got a fair few chuckles.

One aspect to take note of is that none of the comedic elements were malicious or derogatory. You may get some cheap laughs from your close guy mates from doing that but you need to make sure you are catering for all the guests with what you say, not a select few. Unless it's about Auntie Norma's dress - go crazy with that one!

In the thank you to my wife's sister (one of the maids of honour) I took a calculated risk and was a little bit cheeky - see below:

*"Saffron - Helen's sister... I don't normally like to be nice to you. We like to rib each other, we always take the piss out of each other. But I must say despite raising a kid, going to uni, going to work, putting up with Adam, you've still managed to be an awesome sister to Helen. She really appreciates that. It's kind of weird as I haven't actually seen you in a while and it's not because you haven't visited in a while but because normally you are as translucent as a ghost. You've actually got a slight tan today... Sorry about that - I will explain that joke to you later."* ***03:16***

The crux of this joke is that she is super pale-skinned. This could have backfired and you may think it is slightly malicious. However, due to my relationship with my sister-in-law, comments like this are taken in jest - It was and still is, a running joke that I would take the piss out of her lack of pigment.

Therefore, if you have that kind of banter with any of the Bridesmaids, you can take it that little bit further - it got one of the louder laughs of the whole speech with a few shocked smiling gasps - so it was worth it. Actually, come to think of it - now that her fake tan has rubbed off, I haven't seen her for a while again - I have no idea if she is angry or not?!

A word of warning, it is not recommended to do that type of joke with someone you don't have that kind of relationship with. Try to avoid getting punched on your wedding day.

To end this section you want to get the guests to raise a glass to the Bridesmaids but explicitly make sure they stay seated - the only standing toast will be to your wife. Keeping everyone seated will also mean less disruption and is a clear indication that the speech isn't over and you have plenty more to say.

So right now, with your notepad or device - write down the names of each Bridesmaid and a few words of what you want to say about them. If possible add a funny story or characteristic of theirs - if not, consult your wife-to-be for some material. Easy! We will review the bullet points you have made in Chapter 9.

In my speech, I moved on to the Groomsmen.

# Chapter 5 - Recap

- Don't use a generic thank you and "don't they look great" for the Bridesmaids
- Address them individually
- Think of observations you have had of your wife with those Bridesmaids
- Ask your wife for speech material if you are struggling
- Take a risk with some jokes if you have a good relationship with that person, especially if its Aunt Norma
- Raise a toast to the Bridesmaids but get the guests to remain seated

# CHAPTER 6
## THE GROOMSMEN

The Groomsmen are likely to be your best friends and closest family. They have been with you through the best of times and the worst and supported you in many ways. They will also have been complete knob heads to you at some point in your life - now is the time to get your own back.

Just like the Bridesmaids, you want to initially thank them all as a group but name them individually. It's also a good chance to mention the Stag Do and that they made sure you survived.

Maybe leave out the bit about being beaten with a belt buckle by the stripper out of the speech. The Stag group remembers it and will never let you forget it. The scar on your arse will not allow you to forget either.

I digress.

I have heard a speech where the Groom mentioned how drunk they were on the Stag or some sort of other in-jokes. This is lazy storytelling that may get a few chuckles from those who were on the Stag do, but will leave the other guests feeling confused and even excluded.

In-jokes are a surefire way to get the rest of the audience disinterested in the remainder of the speech - always think about keeping them engaged. You want everyone laughing at your Groomsmen, not just a select few. Sorry, I meant *with*, you want them laughing *with* your Groomsmen.

Here is my Groomsmen opener:

*"So we've got the groomsmen - Sam, Matt, Gregg, Nick, Dave, Tom - the most boring British names of all time - and Rob I include myself in that. You are awesome, you got me back home from my stag I really do appreciate it"* **04:29**

Quick, simple, with a little joke about our boring names thrown in there too. You really can't get more boring than those seven names can you?

Next, I moved on to thank each of them individually.

I had one Groomsman who was stuck in the US and unable to attend, so knowing that this was going to be filmed and seen by him, I wanted to make sure he was still included.

*"You will notice that one of the names that I called out, Sam - he isn't here. He couldn't come here to do visa issues. He is not allowed out of America - who knows why. Normally I would disown him as a friend but we are going to America in September and I need free accommodation. So we are going to keep that link."* **04:47**

He appreciated getting a mention in the speech when he watched the video, and the final line got some chuckles. If any Groomsmen or Bridesmaids are missing on the day, don't forget to give them a mention. They will appreciate it.

Once, the missing Groomsman was covered, I moved on to those who were in attendance on the day.

Before I advised that you should not use in-jokes, but in one instance I decided to break that rule:

*"Nick Pointing - thanks for coming today mate."* **05:46**

This was a friend who was notorious in our group for missing social events - so initially this got a few laughs from those friends who knew that, however, to include everyone, I quickly followed up with:

*"He missed his own 30th birthday by the way. So yeah I am really surprised you actually turned up"* **05:51**

An in-joke can work if you follow it up with a swift explanation for everyone else. If it requires a long explanation then don't use the in-joke. Simples.

## The Best Man

The Best Man, of course, needs a special mention. You appointed him to this position as you trust him to deliver a good speech, a memorable Stag Do and be there as support on the actual wedding day.

He will likely be your best friend or brother, so has known you for a long time, usually longer than you have known your wife.

Therefore it is definitely worth getting some heartfelt words in the section that you thank them. Here is an excerpt from my speech:

*"Lastly we got my main man Dave... you've had a bit of a tough year but you've literally been there for me. You organised some amazing stag dos. I know there are quite a few lads here who had a really awesome time. You have done a really good job"* **06:19**

It's not often you give your pals appreciation so use the opportunity of this speech to do just that.

However, you don't want to make it too soppy now, do you? Save that for the wife.

So end your thank you to the Best Man by making a harmless joke about him in some way or form. As his speech was coming up next I went with:

*"My only thing with Dave is is that he is an absolute pathological liar, so please don't believe a word he says after my speech."* ***06:43***

This was clearly all in jest and with the humorous tone set throughout the speech up to that point, the guests knew this. Anything Dave was about to say was pretty much one hundred per cent true, especially the embarrassing stories! Thanks for that mate!

Again, just like the Bridesmaids section, you want to raise a toast to the Groomsmen but you want people to remain seated.

I wanted the toast to the Groomsmen to be a special one, so our party favours on the table were a colourful shot of flavoured vodka in a nice Kilner jar the guests could keep once drunk (we gave our designated drivers / sober friends alcohol-free shots, so they could also get involved).

I took the opportunity in the speech to get the guests to drink that shot in honour of the Groomsmen.

This is a way of using props in your speech as well as getting everyone involved in doing the same action - after everyone did the shot there was a ripple of conversation amongst tables due to the shot strength - so it got people talking/gagging as a result.

If you can have something on the table the guests can get involved with, this is a great way to maintain that engagement.

Now you know what to do for the Groomsmen section - get that notepad or device out. Write down each of their names and jot down a funny story about them or why they have been a good friend to you. Remember don't be too kind to them (they definitely won't be when it comes to their turn) but do be wedding appropriate.

Bridesmaids - done. Groomsmen - done. Let's see what you should include in the Parents' section in the next Chapter.

# Chapter 6 - Recap

- Don't say how drunk you all were on the Stag Do or use any in-jokes - they exclude people
- If you do want to use an in-joke, give a quick explanation for the other guests so they can join in with the joke
- If the in-joke explanation is too long - don't include the joke at all
- Make sure there is a special mention for the Best Man
- Make a joke about how he likes to lie - this tees up his speech perfectly
- If you can - use props that are on the table - an alcoholic shot for everyone works a treat
- Raise a toast to the Groomsmen but get the guests to remain seated

# CHAPTER 7
## THE PARENTS

The parents are probably the most important guests at the wedding.

It is many a parent's dream to watch their child get married and in most instances, they contribute a lot to the day, whether it be financially or by other means.

This is a fact that has to be acknowledged. It will be expected by the parents themselves, your wife and the rest of the wedding guests.

Parents can sometimes be a tricky subject and can all depend on your personal experience, relationships and situation. Both sets of parents might be together, one or both sets may be separated, there may be step-parents involved, new partners, foster parents, etc. It can get quite complicated - trust me.

Therefore I feel the best approach to take is using the same tactic as the Bridesmaids and Groomsmen - thank them individually.

This avoids any awkwardness and each parent will feel individually appreciated. I am sure that whatever your situation is, all parents have been there for you in one way or another and that is exactly what you are going to talk about in this section.

Both sets of parents have more than likely supported you financially during your lifetime if not the wedding itself. If they have financially contributed to the wedding you must say thank you for this - that is simply polite to do so and expected. I would advise doing this part before you move on to each parent individually.

Something along the lines of:

*"Thank you so much to John and Sally for your contribution to the wedding, it simply wouldn't be the day it is without your help"*

If they contributed to something specific then mention that - it will be appreciated.

If you have any gifts to give to people as a thank you, I would advise giving these to the recipients before or after the speech. Gift-giving causes disruption and can ruin the flow of a speech. However, if you feel you can work gifts into your speech seamlessly then go for it. They could even be a prop that forms part of the speech.

I started the parents' section with my wife's parents seeing as it's your speech you will likely want to end the section on your own parents but it is totally up to you.

## Wife's Parents

What is the best way to ingratiate yourself into the family you are marrying into?

By blowing them out of the water with the best Groom's speech ever and being a son-in-law they want to brag about. Imagine being the shining example of a great person your in-laws admire - you can't put a foot wrong ever again. This speech can achieve that! Ok well, maybe it won't go that far but it can put you in their good books for the rest of that day at least!

You may not know your wife's parents all that well and so, similar to the Bridesmaids, have a think about the observations you have had of them and whether you have heard any stories about them that are wedding suitable.

If you are still struggling for material then, again, simply ask your wife-to-be on what she thinks you should say. She is an extremely useful resource!

Below is what I said about my wife's mother:

*"Lorraine - you never fail to make me feel at home when I come to visit you. You always manage to see the best things in life."* ***08:27***

This is a true observation of the time I spent with her. I also followed it up with a funny story my wife told me about her - when she was growing up, her mum would laugh at Helen and her siblings whenever they tripped over.

I found this hilarious and it resonated with me as I can imagine I would be like that as a parent. It was shared humour which luckily the rest of the guests found funny.

As I've said, your future wife is a great asset for speech material and can provide some superb stories!

When I moved on to my wife's father I actually broke my own cardinal rule - I used a joke I had found on the internet. Shock!

The reason for using the stock joke was twofold - I had never heard it before at a wedding (and I have been to a shitload) and it didn't sound too cliché:

*"Brendan, you said it would be the happiest day of my life, and you were right, the Stag Do was insane."* ***08:57***

I am a big fan of this joke and if you think you haven't heard it before in a speech, throw it into your own for guaranteed lols!

The reason I like this joke is that it is a classic disruption of expectation. If your guests' mental momentum is going one way, a good punchline flips it. The element of surprise is fundamental for a great joke. I use this tactic a few times throughout the speech and I will highlight another example later.

As soon as that joke was delivered I moved on to the story of me going to ask the Father of the Bride for his daughter's hand in marriage. This is a safe route to use and if the story is funny then even better.

If it isn't a funny story then you can simply say something along the lines of:

*"When I asked for your daughter's hand in marriage I could sense a tone of relief - someone actually wanted to marry your wayward daughter! I promise to look after her to the best of my abilities - she is in safe hands."*

This ticks the humour box as well as allaying any concerns the father may have as you promise to look after his daughter.

## Your Parents

Now moving on to your own parents, you should

have a fair bit to say about them.

You want to thank them for everything they have done for you throughout your lifetime. I also went down the route of saying what aspects of my personality I got from each parent (I say each rather than both, as I had two step-parents to talk about as well!)

The personality aspect is a good way to think of material for what you are going to say, and it is a way of complimenting them for who they are as a person and what they do. Here are a couple of examples from my speech:

*"Derek - you didn't have to, but you have pretty much treated me like a son, you are generous and the most sarcastic person I know. You literally provided days and years of entertainment teasing Pippa. You have passed that on to me and I just tease Helen all the time. She is always super appreciative of that"* ***10:52***

*"Heather - you are compassionate, loyal, generous. You go far beyond what is expected of you as a mother to all four of us and we really, really do appreciate that."* ***11:34***

The above is what I said about each step-parent.

For Derek, I appreciated his humour, how he

used to wind up my sister and how that had rubbed off on me teasing my new wife a lot. It brought several people into that speech element just from one sentence - try and do that where you can.

For Heather, I recognised her genuine compassionate personality and a few other nice traits. In my original draft of the speech, I thought it would be funny to say I had identical personality traits. You will notice in the excerpt above and the video that I never actually managed to get the joke element out.

This is where I just want to mention that it is ok if you don't remember all your written down speech - as long as you get the key elements in, it will still be successful.

I was a little annoyed with myself for not saying that joke, but in the end, no one noticed and it was a nice appreciated part of the speech that didn't need a joke to conclude.

For my mum and dad, I went for a similar style of mentioning the personality attributes I had inherited from both of them.

*"Mum - you literally did everything for me as a kid. You cut my pizzas into pizza slices, gave me some smiley faces on the side. Really nutritional food - probably why*

*I am so big and strong now. You are super laid back, chilled and easy going and I think that I get those traits from you for sure."* **10:04**

*"Dad - your sociable and hard-working ethos have made me also super hardworking. Everyone knows me as a hardworking guy."* **11:15**

This is a good way to compliment your parents - and yourself!

As I mentioned before, your parents may have not only contributed financially to the wedding but also in other ways. In my situation, we asked my mum to paint some pictures of places my wife and I had visited together, which we put in photo books on each table.

If a parent or anyone has made something or done something special for the wedding, mention it and point it out for all the guests to see and appreciate.

*"Mum...I certainly don't have your artistic flair. If you look on each table at the numbers there is a painting that my mum did of where me and Helen went - so if you get a chance have a look. They are absolutely incredible. Actually, I am going to give you a round of applause for them"* **10:33**

As you can see I kept on the personality trait line for consistency but then mentioned one skill of hers I definitely do not possess. This allowed everyone to look on each table at her talented artistic creations. This involved all the guests, as after the speeches they went to each table to look at the different books.

For the continued flow of the speech you can raise a toast to the parents as a collective, but again make sure it is a seated one to avoid disruption.

Phew - Parents are happy and now you are the model son and son-in-law that the other siblings are envious of. Nicely done!

## Missing Friends & Family

Unfortunately, in many instances, there will be a family member or a friend who is no longer with you. As a Groom, whether it be a relative or friend of yours or your wife's, you should take a moment to mention them. It is likely that a number of guests would have known that person too, and so they will appreciate that you have taken the time to allow them to remember those who are missing on the day.

When it comes to mentioning missing loved ones within the speech, keep your tributes towards the end of the section that person would have been mentioned in. This is so you don't get choked up too soon, which may make you struggle with the rest of the speech.

If you feel that you are about to cry, I have heard that looking upwards can help prevent you from tearing up - don't be afraid to cry though - a wedding is an emotional day, so let it all out.

Take a moment to compose yourself - clear your eyes so you can continue to see your prompt cards and move on to the next section of your speech.

The Father of the Bride may very well pay tribute to missing family members as it's quite traditional, so you may wish to leave it as just the one general tribute, saying something along the lines of:

*"... and we also remember those family members who are no longer with us who would have undoubtedly enjoyed this wonderful occasion."*

Again, if you decide to use the general line above, there may be a few guests upset, so give them and yourself a moment to pause and reflect before you move on to your next part of the speech.

Just like the Bridesmaids and Groomsmen - get your pen and paper or device out and write down each of the Parents' names. Write down any specific contribution they have made to the wedding, what you are thankful for after all those years of looking after you, and how the in-laws welcomed you into their family. Any funny stories here are a bonus - the focus is the thanks and making sure you go down as a certified legend for all future family gatherings.

Now you have thanked all the guests and given special mention to the Bridesmaids, the Groomsmen and all the Parents. That only leaves one person remaining, your wonderful new wife!

# Chapter 7 – Recap

- If they contributed financially to the wedding - explicitly thank them for this
- If complicated family set up - thank each parent individually - possibly do this even if it isn't complicated
- Use stories you have heard from your partner to talk about the in-laws
- Use the asking the father-in-law's permission to marry his daughter story - it's a classic
- If a parent has contributed to the wedding non-financially make sure this is acknowledged too
- If there are any missing friends or family that would have been at the wedding make sure you take a moment to remember them and mention them in your speech so others can share that moment
- Raise a toast to the parents but get the guests to remain seated

# CHAPTER 8
## THE BRIDE

You have made it to the big crescendo! This will be the final section of your speech so let's make it a good one.

But take a moment - don't go straight into the soppy stuff - as you have a good chance to throw in a bit of comedy between the last section and this one. I went with the following:

*"I guess that just leaves one more person. Funny, gorgeous, sexy, generous - those are just some of the words I heard people saying about me earlier - so thank you to all you guys!"* **12:09**

Nothing like a bit of over-the-top arrogance!

Very similar to the father-in-law joke earlier - where you take the guests' mental momentum thinking you are describing your new wife and flip it to being about yourself. Again, this was a quick sentence that got a lot of laughs. Feel free to use it if you can! However, like the joke before, if you and your friendship group have heard something similar then you don't want to overuse it. Be the original and best.

When you start prepping what you are going to say about your new bride, try and avoid all the cliché phrases of "funny, beautiful, kind" as all

Groom's say that about their new wife. And if you think the opposite, that she is "not funny, ugly and cruel", probably best not to get married!

I must admit, I did use a couple of the nice cliché terms right at the start, but then the key difference is I progressed to describing characteristics that make her unique. This allows other people to connect with you as the speaker as they also know those to be her characteristics.

I read on an online Groom's speech tips page that you want to keep your stories short and not too embarrassing when it comes to the focus on your partner. I don't necessarily agree with that - yes stories should be short on the whole but in my opinion, they can also be a little bit embarrassing.

You are marrying someone you have no doubt spent a lot of time with and there should be some funny stories you can tell. Maybe she even has some funny habits you want to share.

Have a little think about what you want to share with your guests and what is acceptable.

There is a fine line between an embarrassing story and a humiliating one, so take some time to think about whether the story will make your new wife blush and laugh or make her angry. Again, try not to get punched on your wedding day!

At this stage you should run what you are going to say past your Best Man - he should be able to give you some advice on the appropriateness and make sure it's just embarrassing rather than humiliating. Unless he is out to sabotage your speech so his one sounds better! Be on your guard - trust no one. Or maybe do just trust him as he is your best mate. Your call.

My wife and I have a relationship where we always tease each other and so I decided to tell a couple of stories about that:

*"We are stupidly silly all the time. You are going to hate me for this, but I am going to give a couple of examples; When I am innocently trying to do my teeth before bedtime she will literally come up behind me and pull my shorts down. I don't know if you have ever tried to brush your teeth and pull your shorts up at the same time. It is impossible. That's a once a week occurrence. Girls do that to your lads this evening.*

*This one time I created a pillow-shaped Rob in the bed and then I hid in another room. So she is brushing her teeth chatting away to this pillow Rob, and I am in the other room giggling away. Then she got into bed with the pillow Rob and I jumped out and scared the shit out of her."* ***13:54***

I thought it would be funny to share a couple of pranks - one she has done to me and one I did to her - both quite harmless.

When it came to describing the de-kegging of my shorts story I also did the actual physical action of trying to pull my shorts back up while brushing my teeth. This added visual emphasis and created a funny observation for your guests and made me look like a fool - all great speech material.

After the prank story, I had a prop ready for the next part (I wasn't done with the embarrassing!).

A lot of the time people can switch off when they are just listening so providing a visual aid engages your audience, especially at this stage of the speech when you have been speaking for around 10+ minutes.

My prop was a simple photo book of screenshots of some of our text messages between each other - highlighting some of the silly nicknames she had given me over the years. This was then circulated around the room after the speeches for the guests to look through at their leisure.

Your prop could be anything at all. For example, she might have a cuddly toy from when she was a child she still sleeps with that you could show your guests, or maybe a weird lucky charm - the possibilities are endless. Have a root around your fiancée's stuff - If she asks what the hell you are doing, just say - "research".

With my prop, I used the photo book to read out some of the nicknames she has given me over the years, of which "Frog" was a common theme. With this element I got lucky as I was able to go down the classic fairy tale storyline:

*"So I'm hoping, like in the classic fairy tales, that kiss we had up there - the frog will now become your prince."*
***16:16***

An extremely cheesy line which got some awws, groans and chortles - nothing wrong with a bit of cheesiness now and then! I think I even told the caterers to cancel the cheese board after that brielliant joke! Sorry cheese puns can be quite grating. I promise I will stop now.

Once your comical elements are done you need to now fully focus on your feelings for your new wife. This is a once in a lifetime opportunity to say how much you love her in front of all your friends and family - so make it genuine and from the heart.

Soppiness warning! :

*"You are unbelievably stunning... I fancy every inch of you. What you think are your imperfections are my perfections. You are loyal, you are caring. Your job at work is literally helping people - you bring that home apart from when I'm being a drama frog... You are generous, ambitious and you just make me a better person. You are my best friend and I literally can't wait to go travelling, buy a house, get a puppy and a kitten."* ***16:58***

This was the penultimate outpouring of heartfelt words - I did manage to fit in a reference to frog again to turn people's smiles into a little chuckle and then ended this sentence with an aspiration my wife and I have to travel the world, buy a house and get some pets. Try and memorise these heartfelt words - it doesn't seem quite as sincere when you are seen reading off the prompt cards.

So the key is to say something amazing but also unique about your new wife while keeping it personal to your relationship. Stock Groomsmen speech words won't cut it here I am afraid and are a surefire way to get in your new wife's bad books. Save that for the honeymoon at least!

Also, if down the line she ever says you never say nice things - then you literally have a recorded reference of you doing so! How convenient. You could even timestamp it and have it on your phone ready to go if you get into a disagreement. Life Pro Tip right there! However, disagreements are unlikely after you have just given the perfect Groom's speech.

This outpouring of feelings for your new wife is the perfect closure to your speech and will lead very nicely into the final toast:

*"And on that note can I ask for you all to be upstanding this time to toast my wonderful new wife!!*

*Cheers!!"* **17:43**

And there you have it - you have completed your speech! You can take a huge sigh of relief, grab that bottle of beer or glass of bubbles and relax as your Best Man takes the reins. Well, I say relax - that all depends on what he has in store for you!

Now is your chance to grab that notebook or device and write down at least three unique characteristics you love about your wife-to-be. Then have a think about any funny, wedding-appropriate stories or habits she has that you can mention. Try and think of three again. Then jot down how you want to finish this section and raise the toast.

So you have read the tips and seen real-life examples for each section of the speech. I am hoping you have noted down a few ideas, some stories, and a few jokes that you wish to include in your own speech, but what is the best process to tie this all together?

Chapter 9 addresses this.

# Chapter 8 – Recap

- When thinking of compliments to say about your new wife think of unique ones for her
- Think up some funny stories or pranks you have played on each other - make sure they are wedding appropriate though
- Make sure you have some heartfelt words towards the end and leave any jokes out of that last bit
- Raise a toast to your new wife and get all the guest to be upstanding this time - your speech has ended!

# CHAPTER 9
## SPEECH PLANNING

## Key points

So right now you probably have a bunch of bullet points either written down or on your device. Give yourself plenty of time. You need at least a month to prepare as there will be multiple revisions required. Yes - it's back to the school homework days I am afraid.

You will have a fair bit of material to organise, but let's recap on what you should have right now and then we can move on to how to prepare for the speech:

- Bridesmaids - List each of their names and any observations you want to say about them or anything your future wife wants you to say
- Groomsmen - List each of their names and why they are your best friends or any funny short stories you have about them
- Parents - List each of their names and what you are going to thank them for
- Bride - List of her unique traits that are why you love her, any funny or embarrassing stories you have and an idea of how you want to end the speech before the toast

## First Draft

Once you have all your material helpfully bullet-pointed it is time to make the first draft of your speech. It doesn't matter which section you start with first. You may find it the easiest to start with the Groomsmen as you know them well, so begin there.

However, at the end of the process, you want a couple of sides of paper per section filled with the constructed sentences and written how you will speak and deliver it.

It is important to write the speech how you would say it, as the guests aren't going to read your speech, they will be hearing it from you, so try not to make it too formal if you aren't a formal person.

Just to caveat that though - you will be speaking to a whole range of people and ages so try to avoid being that diamond geezer you normally are with your mates down the pub. Find a balance. Think James Bond smooth operator, and Indiana Jones cavalier adventurer but still pretty suave. Those two combined = perfection.

Once you have the sections done you can then write your opener - it is easier to write the opener once you have the other sections completed.

## Structure

Once you have all your sections written - think about your structure - you may want to follow the same order of sections I did or be different, but always end on your Bride! I have been to some weddings where they end on the Best Man - I know you love the guy but you haven't just married him. Although at my wedding, some questionable photos made it look like I did.

When you establish the order, you want to make sure the opener links well and the closing toast also links to the last section.

You should now have a full speech drafted.

## Read, Read, Read!

There is one very simple rule - you have to read and reread your speech multiple times. This will allow you to pick up on elements that don't flow and material you initially thought would go down well, may not after a second or third read-through.

Your hilarious made-up joke about how tight the in-laws are may have seemed like a side-splitter when you first wrote it but now a wedding-ruiner on a second read-through.

I removed a lot of material during this phase. I would have been interested to see how the original material would have gone down - but sometimes you have gotta know when to fold!

This phase also allows you to add a lot of new material in, as you aren't going to be able to think of everything in your first draft.

Conversations may come up that give you a lightbulb moment and you have to jot down some alterations to the speech. Add these to your bullet-pointed notes for easy reference.

This is encouraged, but not advised a day or two before the wedding. This is going to jumble your thinking on the actual day. Jumbled thinking = jumbled talking.

Once your prompt cards are written, try not to change anything unless extremely essential.

## Read Aloud, Read Aloud, Read Aloud!

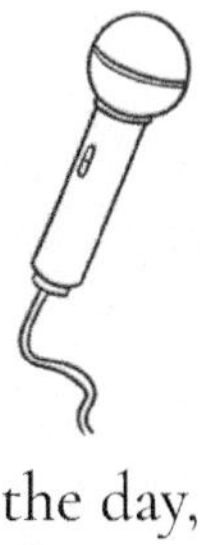

Next, you have to read your speech aloud - this can be to the Best Man or another friend or like I did, just to myself. Don't run through it with your wife though - you want your speech to be a surprise on the day, plus she will tell you to remove some of the more risqué content - you want to keep most of that in. Run those bits by the Best Man.

I said my speech out loud on multiple occasions and recorded myself for playback.

Yes - everyone hates the sound of their own voice, but this is a necessity. I feel like I sound a bit like Jack Whitehall - so a silver-spooned posho - not ideal. Recording it has to be done though. It will allow you to play around with the tone, speed and pitch of your voice in certain areas of the speech, so you can perfect the delivery - especially for the joke punchlines.

## Prompt Cards

When you are happy with the speech, spoken it out loud many times, and have largely memorised it, then you can reduce it down to a few reminder sentences.

This is similar to revision cards you may have done in preparation for exams. I did tell you your school days are back! You can buy blank postcards or specifically made speech prompt cards, and this is what you should bring with you on the day.

There is nothing worse than seeing someone pull out a creased bit of lined paper for their speech and read from it line by line - nothing you say will feel authentic and the listeners will get bored very quickly. You also look like a kid in primary school reading out his favourite hobbies in front of the class - not very James Bond now is it.

I advise having one prompt card per section with keywords written on it. Prompt cards are just that - they are there to prompt you so don't write too many words down as you will rely on them. You want to have practised the speech so many times that you could do it without the cards. They are just there as a back-up if the nerves get to you.

Here is an example of what I had on the Bridesmaids' prompt card:

> Louise - salon, love of foods

> Jo & Lacey - in-jokes, accents

> Pippa - treated her like a sister, comfort blanket (cuddly)

> Sarah - hen dos, PlayStation.

> Saffron - son, working, uni, ghostly no tan

This may look like a complete jumble of words to you but if you compare it to the full speech in the appendix you will see that it's got all the key elements - their names, so I didn't forget them, and keywords about what I was going to say about that person. That is all you need on those cards!

On the prompt cards, make sure you only write on one side of them. This is so you can pick them up and discard them one at a time once you have completed that section. It is also advisable to number them in the corners - this will avoid any mishaps and keep your speech in order!

Once your prompt cards are written, try not to change anything unless extremely essential.

You are now prepared for the day!

Next up - the morning of the wedding...

# Chapter 9 – Recap

- Collate all your notes and bullet points
- Write the first draft in the style of how you will actually speak it
- Write your opener and your final toast
- Structure your speech - now it is all written you can decide at what stage you want to talk about certain things
- Read, read, read - go over your speech multiple times
- Read aloud, read aloud, read aloud - you may hate the sound of your voice but speaking it out loud will help you practice tone and delivery
- Prompt cards - put each section on one card on one side. Have these in front of you on the day but don't rely on them. Use only short prompt phrases and words

# CHAPTER 10

# THE WEDDING MORNING – TIPS & TRICKS

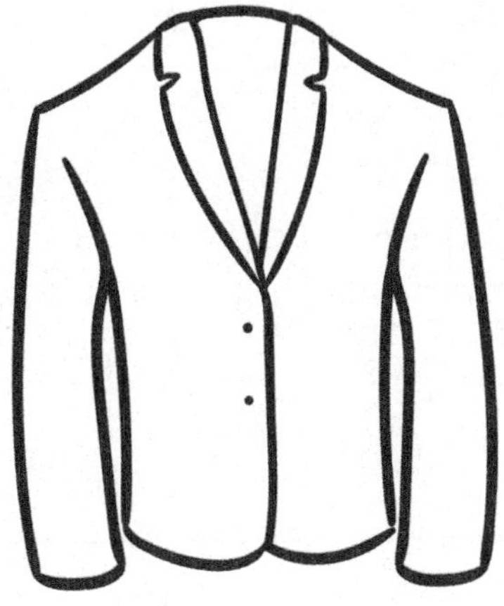

On the morning of the wedding everything is going to go a hundred miles per hour, so here are a few tips to keep you level-headed and make sure the speech goes to plan and you enjoy the day to the fullest.

## Breakfast

It is likely you won't be eating properly until the wedding breakfast which sometimes isn't until late in the afternoon.

Therefore, get something substantial down you as soon as you wake up. My hearty full English breakfast did the trick - just make sure everything on the plate is cooked through. Those are not the shits and giggles you are after!

## Getting Ready

Make sure you have your full wedding suit ready - preferably the night before. Check and double-check that you have the right tie, cufflinks, pocket square etc.

You may also want to double-check with your Groomsmen that they are all prepared - this simple reminder may avoid some embarrassment later during the ceremony.

When getting ready, it's good to have somewhere where all your Groomsmen are with you - they will help settle any nerves. There can be a long wait between waking up and having to put your suit on for the ceremony.

This is, therefore, a good chance to have a couple of drinks - emphasis on the word couple. Too many and the ceremony could turn into a disaster. There is nothing wrong with a little bit of Dutch courage but don't turn into a Dutch Dickhead.

## Essential Items

Make sure your speech prompt cards are with you - they should fit in your suit pocket. Alternatively, if you know where you are going to be reading your speech, you can leave your prompt cards there as long as you know they won't be moved.

Even though you will know your speech off by heart at this point - the prompt cards will give you that conscious safety net.

Next, if you have any props you will be using in the speech - again make sure they are going to be where you need them.

Lastly - the rings - pass over the responsibility of looking after them to your Best Man at the right moment.

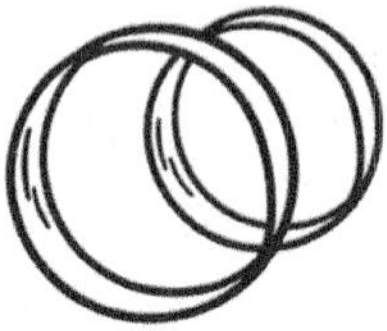

## Show Time

You and your Groomsmen are dressed to impress, you have your speech and props in the right place and the rings are with your Best Man - time to get married! You probably got so engrossed in the speech that you forgot this is what it is all about - get to the top of that aisle and enjoy yourself.

## Pre-Speech

You are likely to be doing your speech after the Father of the Bride - resist the temptation to study your prompt cards. Remember to listen to his speech, as you will be thanking him for it afterwards so you may want to reference something in particular he said.

Take some deep breaths and drink something sweet, which should cure any dry-mouth issues. Avoid alcohol at this stage - you can have that celebratory drink as soon as you are done.

## The Speech

Enjoy yourself - you have done more than most Grooms have by putting in a lot of time, effort and preparation into this Speech. Your wedding guests will love it and feel at ease with you from the get-go.

Raise your glass at the end and take a nice long drink to celebrate your success.

# Chapter 10 – Recap

- Breakfast - make sure you eat something to face the big day
- Getting ready - have your Groomsmen around you and make sure everyone has their outfit sorted
- Essential items - make sure your prompt cards, any props and the rings are where they should be
- Pre-speech - listen to the speeches beforehand, relax, take deep breaths and drink a sweet non-alcoholic drink
- Celebrate when it's done!

# CHAPTER 11

## JOKES TO AVOID

Just for a few laughs, I thought I would list a few of the jokes I found online that made me chuckle but I deemed inappropriate or overused for your Groom's speech - enjoy them here but leave them out of your speech!

All the jokes below I found here:

https://www.hitched.co.uk/wedding-planning/organising-and-planning/groom-speech-jokes/

“Without all of you here today, it wouldn’t be the same…but it would be cheaper.”

“My wife says I never listen, or something like that.”

“All those among you who know my new wife will know that she’s a wonderful and caring person. They deserve a good husband. Thank God she married me before she found one.”

“Before I start, let us observe a few moments’ silence for the countless lilies, roses and carnations that selflessly gave their lives to make this wedding possible.”

“I never actually received a formal invitation to the wedding, so I hope I haven’t just eaten a meal meant for someone else.”

"The buffet this evening is charged on a cost-per-head basis. So, I'd like to thank the following people for not coming..."

"I didn't really know where to start so I thought I'd trawl the internet. After a couple of hours, I'd found some really, really good stuff. But then I remembered that I was supposed to be writing a speech."

"I will shortly be handing over to the best man. But unlike many best man speeches, which are full of sexual innuendo, he has promised me that if there is anything slightly risqué, he will whip it out immediately."

All the jokes below I found here:

https://www.topweddingsites.com/wedding-blog/wedding-speeches-and-toasts/groom-speech-jokes

"Let me tell you that is not the first time today I have risen from a warm seat with a bit of paper in my hand."

"I'd like to thank Mastercard and Visa, without whom this would never have been possible. My wife and I will be forever in their debt."

"My speech today will be like a mini skirt, long enough to cover the essentials, and short enough to hold your attention."

So there you go - don't be tempted to use them but maybe tease your wife that you will be!

# Appendices

## i) Top Tips

Here is a succinct list of all the top tips from each chapter of the book in one easy-to-reference area.

### Key tips for speech content:

- The Groom's speech can be just as funny and entertaining as the Best Man's
- Fail to prepare, prepare to fail
- Have a pen and paper or your phone notes app ready
- You want to try and not go over the same points that those other speeches will
- Talk about each person individually
- Give the guests an insight into your pre-married life
- Don't use a stock joke for an opener
- Don't apologise - it devalues your speech
- Thank all guests for attending
- Build rapport with the guests by finding common ground
- Think of observations you have had of your wife with those Bridesmaids

- Ask your wife for speech material if you are struggling
- Take a risk with some jokes if you have a good relationship with that person
- If you do want to use an in-joke, give a quick explanation for the other guests so they can join in with the joke. If the in-joke explanation is too long - don't include it
- If you can - use props that are on the table - an alcoholic shot for everyone works a treat
- If anyone contributed financially to the wedding - explicitly thank them for this
- If anyone has contributed to the wedding non-financially make sure this is acknowledged too
- If there are any deceased friends or family that would have been at the wedding make sure you take a moment to remember them and mention them in your speech so others can share that moment
- When thinking of compliments to say about your new wife think of unique ones for her
- Think up some funny stories or pranks you have played on each other - make sure they are wedding appropriate though

- Make sure you have some heartfelt words towards the end and leave any jokes out of that last bit

## Key tips for speech creation and delivery:

- Collate all your notes and bullet points
- Write the first draft in the style of how you will actually say it
- Write your opener and your final toast
- Structure your speech - now it is all written you can decide at what stage you want to talk about certain things
- Read, read, read - go over your speech multiple times
- Read aloud, read aloud, read aloud - you may hate the sound of your voice but speaking it out loud will help you practice tone and delivery
- Prompt cards - put each section on one card on one side. Have these in front of you on the day but don't rely on them. Use only short prompt phrases and words
- Breakfast - make sure you have a full stomach to face the big day

- Getting ready - have your Groomsmen around you and make sure everyone has their outfit sorted
- Essential items - make sure your prompt cards, any props and the rings are where they should be
- Pre-speech - listen to the speeches beforehand, relax, take deep breaths and drink a sweet non-alcoholic drink
- Celebrate when it's done!

## ii) Authors Speech In Full

Here is my speech in full. You will see how the written version differs slightly from the video. This was because I ad-libbed various bits on the day and forgot a couple of small items - so don't be afraid to deviate from the written speech - it can add to your connection with your guests.

I advise reading the written version first then watching the video and seeing the difference. You may get ideas on what you could add off the cuff to your speech.

## Rob Bartley - Groom's Speech 02/06/2018:

Video is here:

https://www.youtube.com/watch?v=dxqhNBoYCkY

The original written final draft of my speech is below:

*Hi everyone - hope you are all enjoying yourselves so far. We thought we would kick off the speeches early so here I go!*

*I would just like to say a general thank you to all of you for being here. Some of you guys have travelled far and wide including Manchester and Sheffield from the north and Jersey from the south and even Germany, but special mention has to go to those that have come all the way from the Isle of Wight, so thank you. I know how tough the mainland can be with its big roundabouts and three-lane motorways. But in all seriousness - Helen and I appreciate the time, effort and financial commitments you have made to be here. It is very humbling.*

*Now first the bridesmaids (Sarah, Saffron, Pippa, Louise, Jo & Lacey) who all look fantastic in a great dress which took only 4 months to agree on, I thought it was going to take longer.*

*You have all also kept Helen's nerves at bay and been a great support to her in one way or another in her life and especially the last few months in the run-up to today.*

*Louise - you make Helen look gorgeous every time she goes to your salon and appreciates your mutual love of Craig David shots, cheese and wine and pretty much most other foods.*

*Jo & Lacey - I pretty much have no idea what you 3 are talking about when you all get together there are so many in-jokes, phrases and random accents but I know you never fail to put a smile on Helen's face when you all get together.*

*Pippa - you have taken Helen under your wing and treated her like a sister since day one. I think you may actually like her more than me! But thank you for that and thank you for being a great support to me apart from the times you would hide my comfort blanket (cuddly) or when I bit a chunk out of your shoulder. Now That I'm not 6 years old any more we actually have a pretty good friendship so long may that continue. Love you sis!*

*Lastly - Special mention goes to the two maids of honour; Sarah for organising a couple of fantastic hen dos and being Helen's best friend and confidante all these years. You also have the ability to keep Helen on the phone for a couple of hours at a time so I can play my PlayStation.*

*Helen's sister Saffron, who I don't normally like to compliment as we always tend to rib each other a lot but despite raising a son, working and studying at uni still finds time to be a great sister and support to Helen listening to her many problems. Now, this is actually the first time I have seen Saff in ages. Not because I haven't visited her but because she is normally ghostly translucent and doesn't have a tan like she does today - sorry Saff I tried to be nice and also I will explain that joke to you later.*

*On that note...please stay seated but raise a glass to the bridesmaids! The bridesmaids!!*

*So on to the groomsmen (Sam, Dave, Matt, Tom, Gregg and Nick) with the most boring British names ever. Thanks for getting me back home from my stag do so I could actually get married - it was touch and go.*

*Unfortunately, there is one missing out of that list though, Sam - who couldn't be here due to visa issues and being unable to leave the US. Now if it was anyone else I would probably disown them as a friend for missing my wedding but we are going to America in September and we need the free accommodation.*

*Matt - we have grown up together and you have been a fantastic supporting brother to me. We've shared some awesome times at Centre Parcs and Florida over the years and with an incredible knack for board games bringing out my own inner nerd.*

*Gregg - we share a love for drum and bass and session beers and you can no doubt expect to see me on his shoulders later when a big tune comes on.*

*Tom - you have been a uni friend, a workmate, a flatmate and now my groomsman. Thanks for being awesome and a slight control freak - without you I think our flat and world travelling would have been a shambles!*

*Nick - thanks for coming today. This was the guy who missed his own 30th birthday party about 10 years ago so It was a nice surprise to see you. But joking aside we were next-door neighbours in halls and it was like they matched us on a dating website - Arsenal fan, drum n bass fan and dressing like a chav - it was like we were meant to be.*

*Lastly, Dave - you have had a tough year but you have always found time for me whenever I needed you. You organised and executed amazing stag dos in Hamburg and London which all the lads had a great time and I will be eternally grateful for that. My only problem with Dave is that he is a pathological liar so please don't believe a word he says in his speech.*

*Now you will see that there is a cocktail on your table as your favour. This is delightfully called the Dingle Berry cocktail. It is named after the area in Ireland where we got engaged, Dingle and of course it is berry flavoured. And if you don't know what Dingleberry is please take some time later to google it for the lols.*

*So again remain seated and if you haven't drunk them already please raise your dingleberries for the groomsmen. The groomsmen.*

*Next, I would just like to say thank you to all our parents. Helens first:*

*Lorraine - you have been nothing but accommodating to me and always make me feel at home when I am visiting. You have an incredible talent for seeing the good things in life and not taking it too seriously. Helen told me a story of when her, Saff or Perry used to fall over you didn't have a concern, you just laughed in their face which I thought was hilarious. Although Helen now laughs at me when I stub my toe.*

*Brendan, you told me it would be the happiest day of my life and you were right, the stag do was amazing.*

*But in all seriousness - Brendan you have also welcomed me into the Sheridan family with open arms. I remember I was trying to ask for your permission for Helen to marry me in person when I was in Ryde but I knocked on your door at 11 am forgetting that Saturdays are for Brendan lie-ins so I didn't get a chance to do it face to face. So I had to do it over the phone when I was back on the mainland. I could sense a tone of relief - someone actually wanted to marry your troublesome daughter! I promise to look after her to the best of my abilities - she is in safe hands.*

*Now on to my own parents. I have actually been lucky enough to be brought up by four loving parents. Mum, Derek, Dad & Heather - you have all had a key part in raising the absolute legend and all-round entertainer stood here today.*

*I feel I have received elements from all four of you.*

*Mum - you are selfless, kind, very laidback and don't take life too seriously, traits I feel are some of my best.*

*You raised me to be a gentleman and able to take care of myself and now Helen. However, I certainly don't have an artistic flair like yourself. You will see on each table there is a photobook and in each one there is a painting she did of a destination me and Helen have visited - very talented and thank you for that!*

*Derek - you treated me like a son and provided years of entertainment teasing Pippa, you have made me extremely sarcastic and a constant piss taker - Helen appreciates that a lot.*

*Dad - your sociability and hardworking ethos have rubbed off on me. I'm a sociable guy able to make friends easily and I attribute my success at work to your traits. You had some great stories to tell at the stag do and the lads were intrigued about your former life as a policeman. No doubt there will be more this evening. Thanks for all your support and help over the years.*

*Heather - you are generous not just financially but with your time, you are compassionate and loyal and go above and beyond your duties for all four of us which again are of course traits that we share. Why are you laughing?!*

*I love all four of you and I thank you all for your love and support and welcoming Helen into our large and unusual family!*

*Again please remain seated and raise a glass to the parents!*

*Now I guess that just leaves one more person. Funny, gorgeous, generous, sexy - these are just some of the words I have overheard people saying about me today - so thank you very much.*

*Of course, I am joking - On to my absolutely breath-takingly stunning bride, Helen.*

*You may have already read the how we met story. One element of that describes how only after spending one weekend together, I turned to Tom and said that I was going to marry Helen.*

*Some of you are probably thinking that I said that to Tom after every date but you would be wrong. It only happened three times before at the most.*

*Genuinely I only said it that once as before I had never met anyone I had wanted to marry. In fact, in that one weekend, she had displayed all the traits of my perfect woman and wife.*

*For one she looked like a supermodel and she had the most funny and genuine personality. I was hooked. She took the piss out of me the whole time we spent together and was super sarcastic - a girl after my own heart as I don't take life too seriously and it was refreshing to find someone exactly the same. We are ridiculously silly all the time. Here are two examples; she tries to pull my shorts down when I am brushing my teeth before bed. It's pretty difficult to pull your shorts up with one hand. Girls try this on your fella this evening. Another time I made a pillow-shaped Rob in the bed and she got in just chatting away to pillow me, then I jumped out and scared the crap out of her. Guys if she does the shorts thing you can also try that tonight.*

*She also has some of the most awful nicknames for me. In fact, I have created a photo book of some screen-shots of her texts to me.*

*I am just going to read out a selection of the names she calls me. Nob, you may just think that is a typo for Rob but no it isn't as the next one is nob head, hairy beast, bumder, speccy goober (that one is for when I'm wearing my glasses), vicious little frog, Frogmella, Frog-bert Bartley. You will notice a theme in those last few.*

*Frog as a nickname has come from nowhere but has seemed to have stuck. I mean over the festive period she even wishes me a Merry Frogmas.*

*So I'm hoping, like in the classic fairytales, that after the kiss that sealed the marriage we can retire that nick-name as your frog has now become your prince. Wow - that was awfully cheesy. Can cancel the cheeseboard after that line.*

*But the nicknames just show the kind of silliness we have together every day and what makes spending time with you so enjoyable.*

*I'm usually not very good at telling you how I feel about you so I am going to tell you right now In front of all our friends and family.*

*You are unbelievably stunning, I appreciate and fancy every inch of you. What you think are your imperfections are perfect to me. You are loyal and caring. You help and support people at work and you bring that caring outlook at home too, genuinely helping me whenever I need it unless I'm being a drama frog of course. You are funny and make me laugh every day. You are generous and ambitious and I can't wait to have loads of experiences with you including travelling the world, buying a house and getting a kitten and a puppy.*

*You are my best friend and you make me a better person, I love you more than arsenal, drum and bass and pizza and I will do forever and I am so happy I can call you my wife and we are going to have just the best life together.*

*And on that note can I ask for you all to be upstanding this time to toast my wonderful wife!!*

*Cheers!!*

## iii) Useful Resources

"The Best Man Speaker - The Definitive Guide"
Simon Bucknall

Although this is a book for writing a Best Man speech, Simon has some really useful insights into shaping the humour of your speech, tackling nervousness and public speaking in general. He is an award-winning public speaker so who better to get tips from.

"How To Win Friends And Influence People"
Dale Carnegie

This is a must-read for general life. This will not only make you a better speaker but also an all-round better person that people want to socialise and do business with.

# Acknowledgements

I would just like to thank my parents - June, Derek, Don & Heather for all of your support over the years. I am grateful and appreciative of everything you have done for me. Also thank you mum for proof-reading this book multiple times.

Pippa and Jamie - thank you also for proof-reading and some superb suggestions to add into the book.

Finally, to Helen - you are my everything. Thank you for all you do for me.

Printed in Great Britain
by Amazon

15397515R00078